Susan Perl's
PARK PEEPL

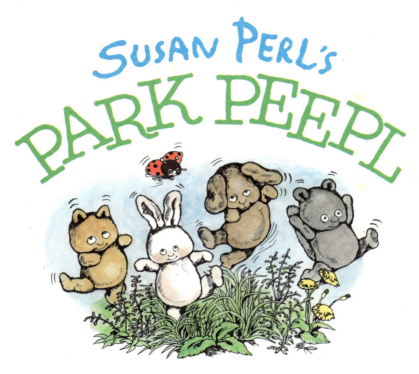

with Verses by Monica Bayley

PARK PEEPL
Text © 1982 Determined Productions, Inc.
Illustrations © 1982 Susan Perl
Published by Determined Productions, Inc.
Box 2150, San Francisco, CA 94126
World Rights Reserved

Library of Congress Card Catalog Number: 81-67306
ISBN: 0-915696-25-8
Printed in Hong Kong
First Edition

PEEPL are people — bugs, animals too,
That means me and that means you.
To be a PARK PEEPL and have fun, too,
Just love the park, that's all you do!

Right in the middle of the great big city,
There's a place all green and pretty.
Bound all 'round by buildings so high,
PEEPL go there to see the sky.

Marmalade's color is sun — not shade,
She loves the park, each hill and glade.

High on the branch of a great big tree,
That's where *Scooter* wants to be.

When it's cold or when it's hot,
The park is *Snuggy's* garden spot.

His ears are big, his tail is short,
Flops is clumsy, but he's a sport.

Lady is a ladybug, you can see,
She's at home in every tree.

We'll go for a walk in our favorite park,
Our trip will last from dawn till dark.

Walking fast or skating slow,
Through the park gate we will go.
Some may follow a piper of tunes,
We prefer the man with balloons.

Flocks of birds are on the wing,
"We are safe and free," they sing.

Some dogs like a frisbee match,
They can't throw but they can catch.

Some horses make us feel quite small,
We don't ride on them at all.

In riding statues we delight,
They don't kick and they don't bite.

Let's find the meadow that once kept sheep,
Our best place to run and leap.

Hooray for greenery! The park has a lot.
It keeps us cool when the city is hot.

If it's windy, fly a kite,
Let out string to such a height.

That planes will swerve and birds beware,
When they find a kite is there.

Once, a turtle beat a rabbit in a race,
Crawling along at a steady pace.
In June, in the park, on a day so rare,
We saw a marathon — won by a hare.

One pursuit on which we dote,
Is bumping around in a little boat.

When the cabbie makes a stop,
We jump in and ride on top.

Actors know they must rehearse,
Reciting Shakespeare in blank verse.

When our trees were looking sickly,
Park officials acted quickly.

Clouds of ladybugs were set free,
To fight the aphids on each tree.

Freed of aphids, see our trees,
Joyful in the summer breeze.

Did you know that our metropolis
Has an obelisk from Heliopolis?

The Met is an opera; the Mets are a team,
The Met in the park is a living dream.

Assembled for our viewing pleasure,
An art museum full of treasure.

We'll view paintings till we drop,
Then we'll go to the postcard shop.

When we try to win boat races,
We make lots of funny faces.

Be nice to pigeons, they're not dumb,
They clean the park of every crumb.

An angel flew across the mountain,
Landed on Bethesda Fountain.

Jumping, climbing, running, crawling,
Sliding, riding, eating, bawling.
Though the playground is a riot,
Mothers get some peace and quiet.

When Big Applers start to swing,
They can do most anything—
Frug or shrug or jitterbug,
Disco dance or bunny hug.

Skaters here, skaters there,
Skaters, skaters everywhere.

Knee pads, shin guards, ankle bracers,
That's what's worn by roller racers.

What we like best, without a doubt,
Are hot dogs topped with sauerkraut.

In a cone or on a stick,
Ice cream is the stuff to lick.

Loudies do not play it fair,
Music <u>can</u> pollute the air.

Litterers put on quite a show,
They're the trashiest bugs we know.

When the carousel goes 'round,
It makes such a lovely sound.

We like to watch the seals cavort,
Gleam and glide, bark and snort.

When the clock is striking noon,
Animals march and play a tune.

Communication in the zoo
Is by squeal or quack or moo,
Grunt or cluck or coo or neigh,
Baa, meow or bark or bray.

Starving artists have to struggle,
Please help those who mime and juggle.

Painting in the park is free,
Because the models charge no fee.

We love parties and receptions,
And their sticky-sweet confections.

Watching from a terrace table,
We're as proper as we're able.

Great big deals are concerts in the park,
PEEPL get there long before dark.

Schlepping along with food and drink,
Every old thing but the kitchen sink.

Drinking, eating, while they're waiting,
Some of them stand up, orating.

When light fades, they are surprised,
To see the stars up in the skies.

All agree by half-past eight,
The overture was worth the wait.

Later, as the notes take wing,
Someone's dog begins to sing.

Now it's night and we're at rest,
Back in the place that we like best.

RESERVOIR

THE GREAT LAWN

Metropolitan Museum of ART

Cleopatra's Needle

DELACORTE THEATER

POND

The Ramble

BELVEDERE CASTLE

BETHESDA FOUNTAIN

Museum of NATURAL HISTORY

The LAKE

TAVERN ON THE GREEN